Aztecs

CONTENTS

© Aladdin Books Ltd

Designed and produced by
Aladdin Books Ltd
70 Old Compton Street
London W1

All rights reserved

Printed in Belgium

ISBN 0-531-17024-1

Library of Congress
Catalog Card No. 86-80623

First published in the
United States in 1986 by
Gloucester Press
387 Park Avenue South
New York NY 10016

Certain illustrations have previously appeared in the "Civilization Library" series published by Gloucester Press.

The consultant on this book, Dr Warwick Bray, is a Reader at the Institute of Archaeology, London, UK.

JILL HUGHES

Illustrated by

DAVID GODFREY, GARY HINCKS, ROB SHONE, JOHN FLYNN AND ROB MᶜCAIG

Consultant

WARWICK BRAY

Gloucester Press
New York · Toronto · 1986

Who were the Aztecs?

The Aztecs were a people who lived in Central America, in present-day Mexico, about five hundred years ago. They were a fierce, warrior people who worshipped terrifying gods – gods that demanded human sacrifice. But the Aztecs were also farmers, merchants and craftsmen, and although they had no wheeled transportation or beasts of burden, the Aztecs created a flourishing civilization.

Before the Aztecs

The Aztecs had been a wandering tribe who reached Mexico, coming from somewhere in the north, in the 12th century. Other peoples and civilizations had lived in Central America before the Aztecs. A powerful race called the Toltecs had built great cities, but these had been destroyed just before the Aztecs arrived in the valley of Mexico.

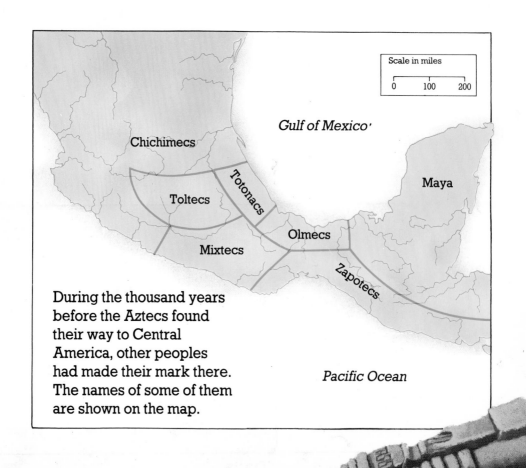

Scale in miles

0   100   200

Gulf of Mexico

Chichimecs

Totonacs

Maya

Toltecs

Olmecs

Mixtecs

Zapotecs

During the thousand years before the Aztecs found their way to Central America, other peoples had made their mark there. The names of some of them are shown on the map.

Pacific Ocean

Above, in Aztec picture language, are members of the tribe wearing clan crests and walking (shown by the footprints) to their new home – which is represented by the "place picture" on the right.

Aztec nomads marvel at the ruins of a Toltec temple.

Settling by the lake

The Aztecs knew they had reached the land promised to them by their god, Huizilopochtli, (whose image they had carried with them) when they saw the valley of Mexico spread out before them.

In their own language, the Aztecs called themselves "the Mexica" and it is from this word that the land of Mexico got its name.

When the Aztecs reached the site of today's Mexico City, they found a valley filled by a huge lake, on whose shores other tribes had already settled. Guided by their god, Huizilopochtli, who spoke to them through his priests, the Aztecs camped by the lakeside. For years they squatted on the land of others until a people called the Colhua granted them some land of their own.

An island home

The land given by the Colhua was rocky and full of poisonous snakes, but the Aztecs ate the snakes and managed to till the poor land. However, the situation changed when they sacrificed a Colhua princess to their god Huizilopochtli. The enraged Colhua drove them from the land into the swamps of the lake.

Here the Aztecs gathered together on an island in the reeds and built mud huts and a temple for their god there. They fished for frogs and worms to barter with. Soon they reclaimed more land from the swamps and the precarious settlement grew larger.

The Aztec state

By the 14th century the island home was not only a flourishing city but had founded a colony on an island nearby, Tlatelolco. The Aztecs were now a serious force and soon began to vanquish rival city-states.

Tenochtitlan was the name the Aztecs gave to their island home. It means "place of the cactus." They used reeds and the silt from the lake to expand their tiny island.

The great city

A huge plaza, or square, at the heart of the city contained the temples of the most important gods, the priests' houses, the court for sacred ball games and the grisly skull rack – built to hold the heads of sacrificial victims.

Two hundred years after the Aztecs had founded their island home, Tenochtitlan, the village in the reeds had become a great city of stone and mud-brick buildings. Instead of roads, the city had canals on which the inhabitants traveled by canoe. The fertile lake mud made excellent gardens in which the citizens grew corn and beans.

By the early 16th century there must have been 150,000 people living in the city. They were governed by a royal ruler and worshipped other gods besides Huizilopochtli, all of them honored with great temples.

The Aztecs' main method of transportation was by canoes through the city's network of canals on the lake. Tenochtitlan was also linked to the mainland by three long causeways. All around the lake were cities either humbled by the Aztec army, or at best uncertain allies. And so, as a precaution against sudden attack, these causeways were spanned by removable bridges.

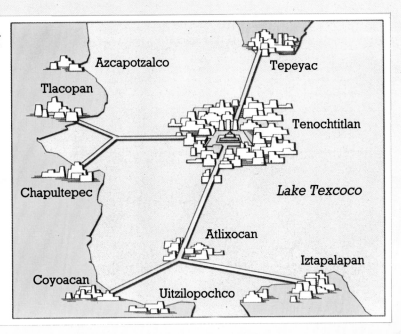

Azcapotzalco

Tepeyac

Tlacopan

Tenochtitlan

Chapultepec

Lake Texcoco

Atlixocan

Iztapalapan

Coyoacan

Uitzilopochco

The Aztec ruler

The ruler was elected and he was always chosen from the royal family. He was the head of the Aztec kingdom and was treated with great reverence by nobles and the people. He ruled with the help of a close adviser called Snake Woman (who was nevertheless a man) and a council of high officials.

The Aztec ruler had to be both brave and wise. He had to lead his armies in battle as well as decide foreign policy toward the Aztecs' neighbors and subjects. One of his titles was *tlatoani,* which means "the one who speaks." His opinion was listened to with awe when he appeared on ceremonial occasions dressed in his finery.

Once a year the Aztec ruler, on the far right, honored his warriors, giving them magnificent feather cloaks, shields and headdresses.

Below the ruler and Snake Woman came a council of military chiefs and below them the knights. Priests and merchants formed classes of their own. The ordinary citizens were divided into clans. Finally, there were a limited number of servants and slaves.

The Aztec gods

The Aztecs' first god, Huizilopochtli, lord of the sun, had been joined by many others by the 16th century. Some of the new gods such as Quetzalcoatl, shown here wearing a jaguar costume, had been adopted from other peoples of the region.

The Aztecs had endured many hardships on their journey to Mexico, and once in the promised land they were still at the mercy of famine, flood and earthquake. It is not surprising that many of their gods reflect the power of the natural world. Tlaloc, the rain god (second left), could make the crops grow. Huizilopochtli, the sun god (far right), was at the center of all life. Xipe Totec (center back), with a flayed human skin, was the god of spring – when the earth grows a new "skin" of vegetation.

This Aztec painting shows Ometecuhtli, father of all creation, clutching the symbol for lightning. Huizilopochtli and Xipe Totec were two of his four sons.

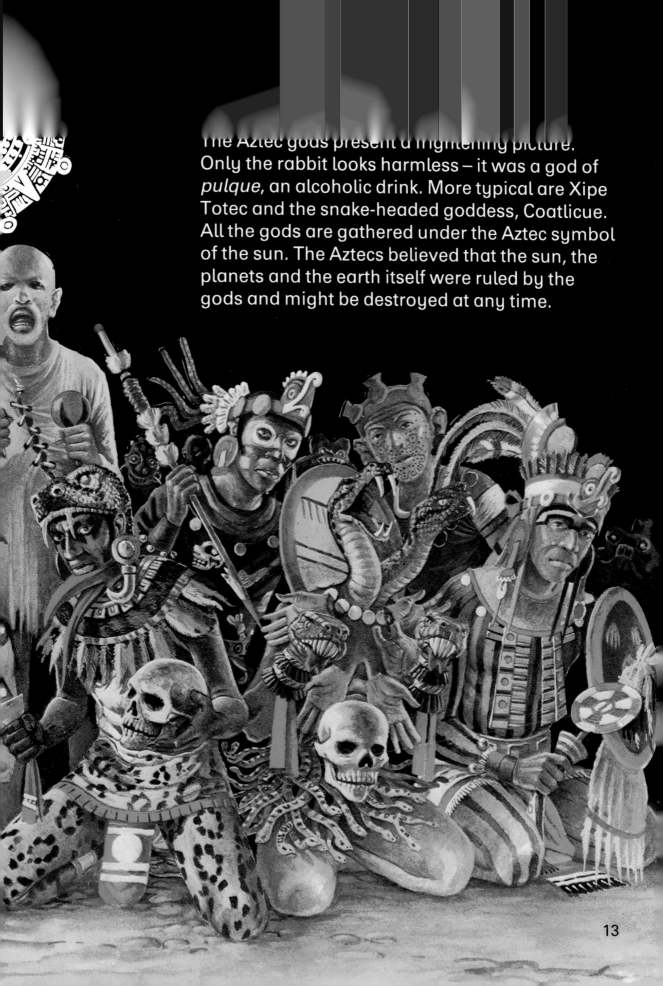

The Aztec gods present a frightening picture. Only the rabbit looks harmless – it was a god of *pulque*, an alcoholic drink. More typical are Xipe Totec and the snake-headed goddess, Coatlicue. All the gods are gathered under the Aztec symbol of the sun. The Aztecs believed that the sun, the planets and the earth itself were ruled by the gods and might be destroyed at any time.

Hearts for the sun

According to Aztec legend, the gods had once sacrificed themselves so that the sun would rise every day and mankind could live. In order to repay the gods, and to ensure that the sun would continue to travel across the sky, the Aztecs sacrificed human victims. Their bleeding hearts were held up to the sun, Huizilopochtli, as a token of Aztec faith.

This seems terribly cruel to us but the Aztecs thought it had to be done if the whole of mankind was to survive. Most victims went willingly to their deaths, considering it an honor. At an exceptional festival in 1487, 20,000 captives may have been ritually killed.

Sacrifices were made with razor sharp knives whose blades were of a hard stone like flint or obsidian.

A captive dedicated to the sun god was given *pulque*, the sacred drink, which probably dulled his feelings. The priest then slashed open his chest and held up his still-beating heart to the sun. This gruesome ritual usually took place at the top of the temple steps.

Religious festivals

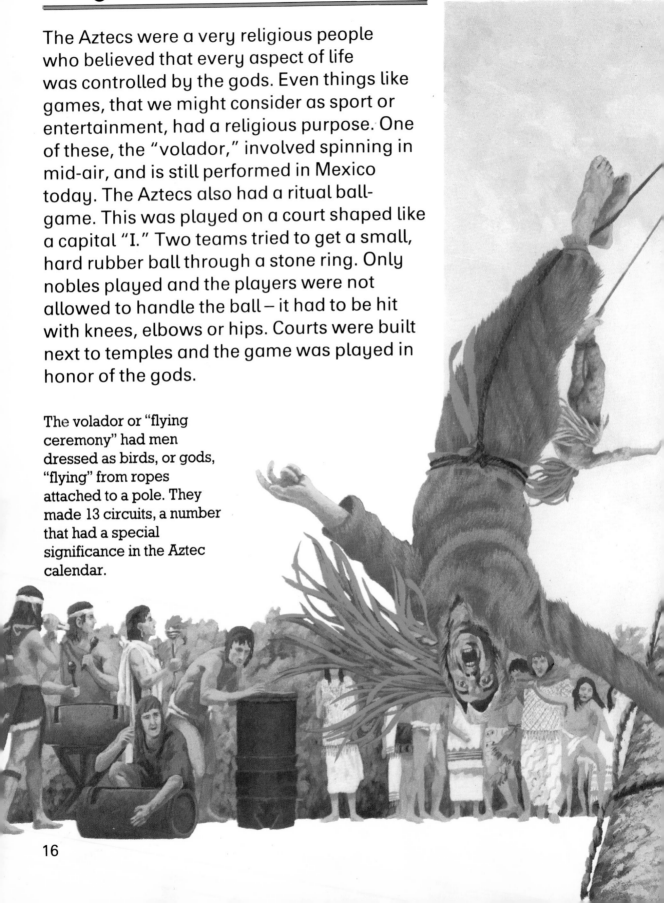

The Aztecs were a very religious people who believed that every aspect of life was controlled by the gods. Even things like games, that we might consider as sport or entertainment, had a religious purpose. One of these, the "volador," involved spinning in mid-air, and is still performed in Mexico today. The Aztecs also had a ritual ball-game. This was played on a court shaped like a capital "I." Two teams tried to get a small, hard rubber ball through a stone ring. Only nobles played and the players were not allowed to handle the ball – it had to be hit with knees, elbows or hips. Courts were built next to temples and the game was played in honor of the gods.

The volador or "flying ceremony" had men dressed as birds, or gods, "flying" from ropes attached to a pole. They made 13 circuits, a number that had a special significance in the Aztec calendar.

Seasonal celebrations

Many religious festivals were linked to the yearly round of spring, summer, fall and winter. When the first green shoots of corn appeared in the spring, a young girl was chosen to impersonate Xilonen, the corn goddess. She was dressed in a feather crown and then treated like a queen for a day and a night. But at the end of her brief reign, the girl was led to the temple of Xilonen and was sacrificed to ensure a good harvest.

Although many religious festivals involved human sacrifice, some did not and most provided opportunities for the people to sing and dance and enjoy themselves.

Turquoise mosaic masks may have been worn by the priests to impersonate the gods during ceremonies.

War as a way of life

From the king downward, Aztec men had to be prepared to fight in battle. Priests and merchants fought. No one could be honored as a nobleman until he had taken captives. The Aztec empire was a loose collection of states that paid tribute to the Aztec ruler and was governed by perpetual warfare. Besides territory and tribute, war provided a constant supply of captives for human sacrifice.

Eagle and jaguar knights played a special part in religious ceremonies, taking part in gladiatorial combats with sacrificial victims who had only plain wooden clubs.

The Aztec army

The Aztec army must have presented an extraordinary sight. Knights wore elaborate costumes of padded cotton "armor," suits of jaguar skin or feathers and huge feather crests. Armed with spears or clubs edged with obsidian, the Aztecs beat drums, yelled and whistled as they advanced.

Knights in cotton armor, wearing eagle and jaguar helmets, lead rows of prisoners back to Tenochtitlan to be sacrificed to Huizilopochtli. Prisoners, rather than corpses, were the objective of Aztec campaigns.

Trade and tribute

These merchants are making sure that the corn cobs they are considering buying are in good condition.

Tenochtitlan remained an island city and, although the citizens grew food in their gardens, many raw materials and other necessities had to be brought from the mainland. Moreover, by the 16th century, Aztec society was rich and had developed a taste for luxuries like cocoa beans, precious stones and brilliant featherwork. Aztec merchants traveled far in search of these and other goods.

Merchant adventurers

Aztec merchants formed a special class, with their own quarter of the city and even their own god. They were often very rich but they were not allowed to display their wealth. They wore humble dress and unloaded their merchandise secretly at night to avoid notice.

Merchants were often the first Aztecs to enter new territories, either as spies for the Aztec ruler, or to establish trading posts in friendly states. They often had to fight for their lives against hostile states.

Tribute arrived in Tenochtitlan by canoe, or was carried over the causeways by columns of porters. Goods offered as tribute to the king were often handed over to his own merchants who traded them for more luxurious items.

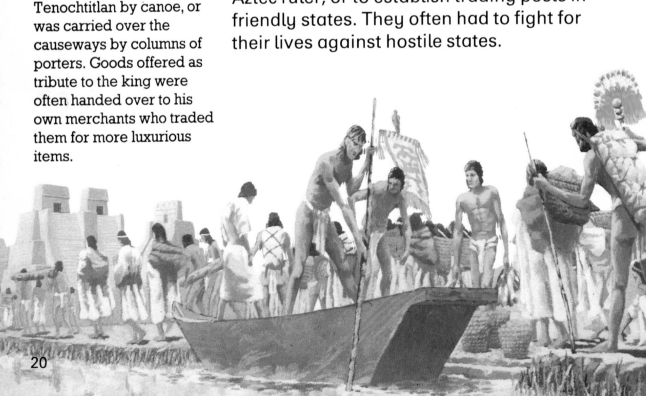

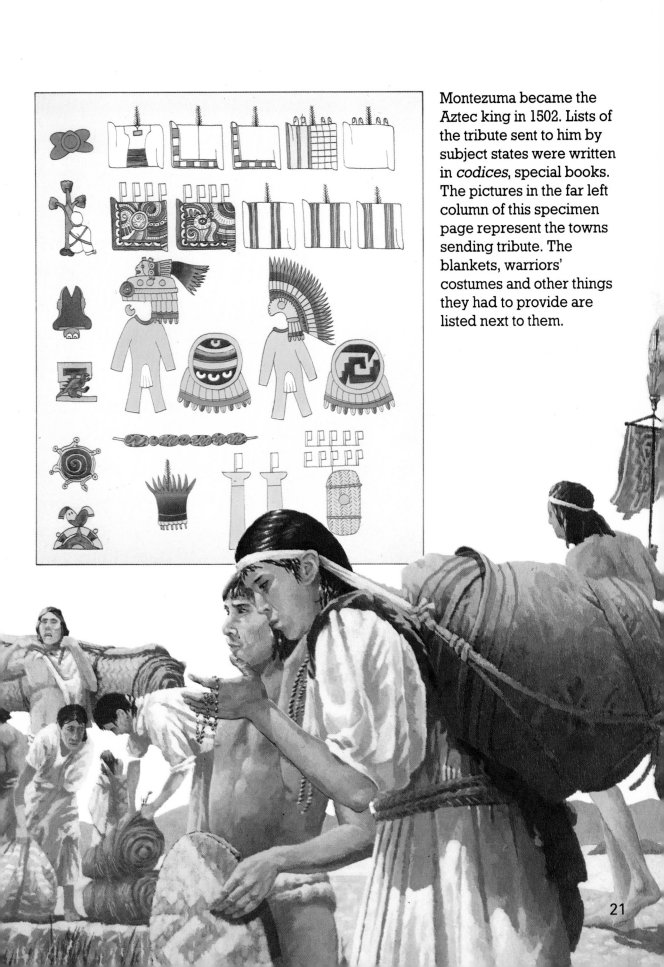

Montezuma became the Aztec king in 1502. Lists of the tribute sent to him by subject states were written in *codices*, special books. The pictures in the far left column of this specimen page represent the towns sending tribute. The blankets, warriors' costumes and other things they had to provide are listed next to them.

The Aztecs did not have money so most goods were exchanged by bartering. Some goods had fixed values that were measured in grains of gold, cocoa beans or cotton clothes. When the Spaniards reached Mexico, in the 16th century, they were amazed at the size and wealth of the market.

The Spaniards saw how the dealers in gold, silver and precious metals were given one section of the market. Another quarter was for the slave dealers, whose human merchandise stood in rows with wooden collars around their necks.

The range of foodstuffs was enormous. Turkeys and dogs were sold for meat and there were fruit and vegetables of all kinds. The Spaniards noted how many different kinds of honey could be bought.

A sample of some of the food eaten by the upper classes indicates just how exotic Aztec food could be. It included venison, chilies, prickly pears, chocolate, crows, pheasants, tadpoles, fish roe, "cheese" made from algae, waterfly eggs and cakes of red worms.

The market at Tlatelolco

Tlatelolco, the second Aztec city, was famous for its great market. It was probably one of the largest in the world, outside China, by the 16th century. Tlatelolcan merchants combed Central America for exotic goods to sell there — embroidered cotton cloths, feathers, jade, gold, vanilla and the valuable cocoa beans from the "hot lands" of the south and east. Local produce, pottery and baskets were there in abundance.

Market rules

There was strict government control over the way the market was run. A court of judges sat whenever the market was held to settle disputes on the spot. Inspectors went among the stalls checking weights and measures.

Boys (far left) went to school, but girls (left) stayed at home and learned women's work, like weaving or grinding corn for flour. A bad boy (bottom far left) was punished by being held over the smoke from a fire of peppery chilies! Another punishment was to prick children with cactus spines. Marriages were arranged by the children's parents. The ceremony ended with the couple "tying the knot" (bottom left).

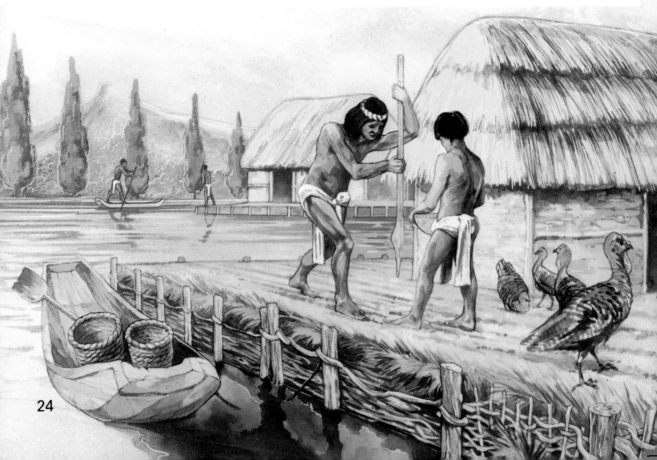

People of Tenochtitlan

Aztec life was not all war and human sacrifice. The ordinary citizens married, brought up children, grew food, fished, wove baskets and cloth. They were organized into clans called *calpullis*. The clan owned the land and ran schools for boys. When a young couple married they were granted a plot of land. Farmers, goldsmiths and fishermen all had their own clans.

Many Aztec small-holdings were built up from silt raised from the bed of the lake. In fact this was how Tenochtitlan expanded. Here, a farmer uses a digging stick while his wife grinds corn. Corn was stored in the circular mud and thatch silos.

Family life

It was a husband's job to build the family house and plant crops on his land. His wife fed any animals they had, cooked, made clothes and looked after the children. Every day corn had to be ground for flour to make *tortillas*, the pancakes that are still a staple food in Mexico today. Boys were brought up to do the same jobs as their fathers.

The Aztec calendar

This huge stone from the temple of Huizilopochtli has the face of the sun god in the center. Signs around the outside foretell the end of the world in a catastrophic earthquake.

The Aztecs were skillful astronomers who studied the movements of the sun, stars and planets. They worked out a solar calendar of 365 days but they also used a sacred almanac of 260 days to calculate the date of religious festivals and to foretell the future.

The Aztecs also interpreted signs and omens. Shortly before 1519, Montezuma, the Aztec ruler, was visited by an eagle with a mirror in its head. In the mirror he saw monsters, half-men, half-deer. It was not until the horsemen of the Spanish adventurer, Hernando Cortés, landed in Mexico a few months later that the omen was understood.

After every 52 years the Aztecs performed a ceremony to celebrate the start of another 52 years of life. When the constellation of the Pleiades reached the center of the heavens, the watching priests sacrificed a victim and kindled a "New Fire."

As soon as the priests had lit the New Fire, runners with torches carried it to all parts of the valley of Mexico.

Only priests were trained to tell the future from the sacred almanac and to advise people on lucky or unlucky days for important decisions.

Gold was only one of the things the Aztecs valued. Cocoa beans, jade and brilliant feathers were worth as much to them. The Spaniards were obsessed with gold, however. They broke into the treasury of Montezuma's palace and found masses of gold ingots, plates and jewelry. These small ornaments are a sad remnant of the once great Aztec treasure.

The Spanish invasion

Hernando Cortés landed in Mexico with 400 Spanish soldiers in 1519. Like other European adventurers he was seeking gold for himself and territory for the Spanish crown. He was so determined to succeed in his mission that he burned his ships before marching inland.

Montezuma did not know what to do. If the Spaniards were gods (as some thought, never having seen men on horseback) he should welcome them. If they were enemies, he should fight. While he was hesitating, Cortés reached Tenochtitlan. He was received with honor by Montezuma and responded by taking the ruler captive and holding him hostage in his own palace.

Cortés left Tenochtitlan, leaving his men on guard. When the Aztecs began noisily celebrating the festival of Huizilopochtli, the nervous Spaniards attacked them and then fled for their lives.

Cortés' men stole as much gold as they could carry but had to throw it away as they struggled to escape through the swamps of the lake.

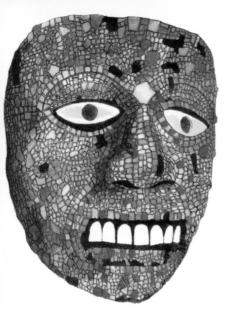

The final battle

Cortés was determined to recover Tenochtitlan. Through an interpreter he gained allies among the Aztecs' neighbors and built small ships that he armed with cannons. Montezuma had been killed in the previous attack. His brother succeeded him but died within four months of smallpox (brought to Mexico by the Spanish.) His nephew Cuauhtemoc led the heroic Aztec resistance to the Spanish siege of 1521.

This mask, a rare survivor of Aztec culture, is in the British Museum, London, UK.

The last stand

Cortés divided his forces into three and advanced up the causeways toward the island city. The fighting was long and bitter but in the end the Aztecs were no match for the armed Spanish troops and their Indian allies. The Aztecs were fatally hampered by their desire to take prisoners in the battle, but their weapons were, in any case, useless against Spanish steel and gunpowder. After 80 days Tenochtitlan fell with perhaps 100,000 of its inhabitants and the Aztec empire was at an end.

Spanish rule

The immediate result of Cortés' victory was the enslavement of the native Mexicans by their conquerors. Spanish settlers took the land. The beautifully worked golden ornaments and statues were not appreciated by the Spaniards, and were melted down into ingots for shipment back to Spain. Priests set about destroying the temples and burning the codices. Scarcely any have survived. Only a band of Franciscan friars who learned the Aztecs' language tried to understand the Aztec culture. Objects in museums and a few archaeological sites are all that remain today of a once spectacular people.

The cathedral in Mexico City is built on the site of and with the stones of the vanished temple of Huizilopochtli. Nevertheless, many traces of Aztec beliefs are still present in the version of Christianity practiced by the Mexican Indians today.

Glossary

Aztec This was the first name the Aztecs had for themselves taken from their first home Aztlan. Later, they renamed themselves Mexica.

Calpulli Clan. Each clan had its own area in Tenochtitlan, its own military leader and its own god.

Codices (Plural of codex.) Aztec "books," written in pictorial symbols on long, folding strips of cloth or paper.

Eagle knights These, along with the Jaguars, fought as an élite in the Aztec army. But they had many religious duties as well.

Obsidian A hard volcanic glass that when flaked has a very sharp edge. It was used for weapons and razors.

Pulque A sacred drink brewed from the sap of the agave plant. It caused drowsiness and dreams and was drunk during religious festivals.

Skull rack A framework filled with the heads of sacrificial victims. The Spaniards saw one with over 100,000 skulls.

Tlatolani Although "the one who speaks" was always a member of the ruling family, he had to be elected by an inner council.

Index

PRINTED IN BELGIUM BY
proost
INTERNATIONAL BOOK PRODUCTION